# BITTERING THE WOUND

# BITTERING THE WOUND

## JACQUI GERMAIN

AUTUMN
HOUSE PRESS

*Pittsburgh, PA*

"Autumn House Press" and "Autumn House" are registered trademarks owned by Autumn House Press, a nonprofit corporation whose mission is the publication and promotion of poetry and other fine literature.

 This project is supported in part by the National Endowment for the Arts.

 Autumn House Press receives state arts funding support through a grant from the Pennsylvania Council on the Arts, a state agency funded by the Commonwealth of Pennsylvania, and the National Endowment for the Arts, a federal agency.

This project is also supported by the Amazon Literary Partnership Poetry Fund and the Academy of American Poets.

Cover art: WANGECHI MUTU. *Riding Death in My Sleep*, 2002. Ink and collage on paper. 60 x 44 in. Courtesy of the Artist.
Cover design by Melissa Dias-Mandoly

ISBN: 9781637680568
LCCN: 2022938584

# CONTENTS

# INTRODUCTION

There were times while reading *Bittering the Wound*, a stunning work of poetry, when I found myself calling it a kind of war correspondence. But Jacqui Germain chin-checks that impulse in "For the Hooked Knife" where she quotes a social media post reading:

*Headed into a war zone. Leaving*
*for Ferguson on Saturday.*

From there, she breaks down the pernicious presumption of the statement. Its willful traffic in danger and allure. Its gaffle of risk, its extradition of Ferguson to anywhere but here in a place some call the US. I, like the person behind the post, was calling out its name. "War," as she writes elsewhere, is a useful term, as the personified injuries of St. Louis's West Florissant are useful, as

how some bodies are
most recognizable when
there is blood, how some body-cities
are only seen when they are screaming.

These bodies and cities, understand, are alive—not merely bleeding, but screaming. And ultimately, despite a history of romanticization, it is difficult to make war be about life. How life matters. And this is a book about the matter of Black life, which may involve standing in a "newly gouged universe" "blistering / with smoke and glass." That such living is to be "a mass of questions marching / across the city, wailing"—any city, any place, really, that pulses under the weight of "America's presumed mercy." The weight of that American presumption is also a matter of Black life, and what Germain does, again and again in these bright, burning poems, is refuse presumption. The specificity with which she renders existing in a state of protest, of action, of shows of strength, seems to me to insist on experience, on the mess of being there, in a place where one must bitterly acknowledge the utility of bleeding. This, too, is a matter of Black life.

Critically, reading *Bittering the Wound* did not allow me to imagine that *I* was there on West Florissant—Germain's specificity refused vicariousness—which made me feel my absence keenly, and offered a vivid sociality with those who were. Germain has neither time, nor, perhaps, the inclination to ask where I was, leaving whatever way that feels for me to deal with. Here's *her* life, alongside others', in a place one might be tempted to call a war zone, but one must certainly call the US. *Every poem* held me right where I was, a place also called the US, but more specifically, in my Black life. And I am grateful to her for that, as grateful as I am for her harrowing actions in that city. Beyond gratitude, however, I feel astonishment for what she demands from her lines, from her sentences, the images she reels, the force of her skepticism, commitment, her love, that she makes it home in a place called the US, that she won't vanish before the headlights in her rearview do.

So, I will not call this war correspondence. I call it a singular work of poetry. I call it an unflinching lyric of living under brutal powers that insist "Black life" is an oxymoron. I call it by its name: Jacqui Germain's *Bittering the Wound*, winner of the CAAPP Poetry Prize.

I call myself lucky to have read it.

—Douglas Kearney
a place some call Saint Paul, MN

# BITTERING THE WOUND

toward a better memory

& for what we lost, learned,
& survived back then

"If, as a human being, you find yourself treated and appreciated less than your surroundings, if you are made to feel that the state will protect glass with more earnestness than your own flesh, mustn't the glass crumble? Mustn't you assert your place as the more essential treasure of this world?"

—Brandon Wilson, 2014

# ON THIS DAY

*for Antonio Martin*

The clouds pulled
apart from themselves
like a damp napkin splitting
its own skin. When it came,
the night brought a pack
of wolves between its gums.

There were at least fifty of us,
the fresh, sickly syncopated
beat of *another one* bumping
through our clammy joints.
The lights of the gas station
turned the scene theatrical,
a cluster of officers lacing navy and black
through the pumps.

An arm and then another arm, someone yanks
a sleeve and a knee bobs toward the pavement,
an elbow pressed against someone's chin
and suddenly, the bodies
are a twist of limbs, slipping
around themselves like a fist
of particles, frantic
and near-materialized,
another creature altogether.

It's December. The news cameras have found
a newly gouged universe
in another city. Humvees in St. Louis
are old news. Always hands
and handkerchiefs. A black person alive
and then not in the tortured pixels
of some video footage. A wall of rubber
and metal rippling across the street.

We, the weary, with our soured nerves
turned rotten and bitter with repetition.

A new gas station dressed in the ash
of the old one. There are no news cameras,
no witnesses. Our anger comes unbridled,
ballooning and buckling against the skyline.
We snarl, snap our teeth, flex our forearms,
pace through the wet grass.

By the time the brawl begins,
it is overdue, already too late
to temper the adrenaline preceding it.
We'd been licking our teeth at each other
for months now, St. Louis and St. Louis again.

The news outlets tongue another
city's cracks, and it's just us now,
the novelty having withered into the winter.
My, my, my—how hungry we've been,
how eroded our faith in whatever mercy
or fear stopped us before now.

A flash-bang erupts and the scattering is reflexive:
my thighs jerk suddenly in the opposite direction.
I lose my left shoe, my breath, everyone I arrived with.
I'm standing on the tar, lopsided. Jarred
but steady now. The wet ground
soaking into my left sock.

And that's it, that's the whole story.

Sometime, before or after, the QuikTrip
across the street was set ablaze & a single cop
sauntered toward the melee with an AR-15
tight against his chest & a friend ran
toward the flames to warn people & I had a vision
of him being peppered with bullets, so I screamed
& cussed him clean the hell out while his jacket vanished
into the crowd

Sometime, before or after, we were arguing
with three police officers anchored in line beneath
the gas station's overhang about this impossibly large,
broken, American *thing* & we were shaking
our hands & they were rolling their eyes & another friend
burst into tears & I'd never seen him cry before & he couldn't stop
& I saw him fighting it, you know, the kind of cry so fresh & foreign
it comes out of a man confused & sputtering & so I hid him
in my shoulder until it passed—but that's it,
that's the whole story. I swear.

# THINE EYES, THINE EYES

*for the street medics, trained and untrained*

Amid the burn, the body, strained
and helpless, leans back beneath
the seamless sky; the soft neck, tender and humming,
unfurls over someone's arm. The wretched,

shouting mixture of anguish congeals
into a whispered tongue, indecipherable
to everyone except the blessing
and the about-to-be-blessed,

a frantic ululation groaning up the throat
as the milky wash or water coats us
in a desperate and haphazard
reach for salvation. Surrender

and be made to see again;
surrender and then blink wildly
skyward; surrender to a filthy
curbside and a stranger's hands.

Does this earn us
heaven? What if this doesn't
earn us any heaven?

# BY THE GRACE OF THE GAZE

What they don't understand is the media coverage became
a             wild thirst, tongue lapping at our rawest edges,
bitter        with our own exhausted attempts to
gift          St. Louis back its own hardened jawline, prepare its skin
to            manage the onslaught—which, well-intentioned or otherwise, will
be            invasive, a conveniently malleable allegory
caught        between book deals and the hungry fascination hidden
beneath       their fingernails, persistent residue coating
the           years since then in a strange spotlight, the magnifying
glass,        an innocent tool until the sun shines through.

# WHAT WE PURGED BEFORE THE FIGHT

Here, a shining simulacrum circled by fire,
an effigy for the parts of myself unable
to survive the culling. Here, the surrender
of all the soft things too dangerous for battle,
too tender to lose to a violent country
that puppets the treasures it exsanguinates.

Here, taste the joy-blessing, the good-warm,
the small, frivolous splendor, the richly flavored
thing I cannot eat. Afraid to waste it
on a mouth like mine, having relieved
the tongue of such pleasurable weight and spat it out
on the sidewalk. Here, the steaming lump
of hot-happy gracing the pavement,
exposed to feet, the August heat, the burning
air, muggy with fists and metal batons
and a salty hate that burns—but for me?

Nothing sweet, nothing grace, nothing
sugar / here, taste the joy-blessing but
do not swallow.

Remember the good-warm though I cannot
keep it. The small, frivolous splendors too heavy
and beautiful to carry into the night.

# FOR THE STREET THAT HELD US

The sun is a low tremor
of light as West Florissant prepares
for the coming quake of bodies.

The street breathes deeply, twists
its sidewalks into an unwelcoming
mouth, and waits for feast.

It begins suddenly, but only
in small licks scarcely enough
to wet its tongue: the rush

of a small group of armored men
across the threshold, the shocked
fluster of our shoulders

brushing through the musty air
for safety or rushing toward
another crowd to become

a bigger mass, if only for these
flash moments of threat
that cut through the night.

Under this moon, this time,
no tear gas for the bodies
daring the army

to flaunt its familiar violence.
This time, the tar tastes mostly of feet
and the worn leather of old fear

that comes shuffling back
through the night and the weeks
and the months, reminding our bodies

of our own flavor, seasoned
and syruped by the St. Louis summer.
A handful of protesters move

too fast and West Florissant flicks
its wrist. The police line shudders,
and I slide my kerchief over my mouth and nose.

The street opens its jaws, expecting
the hovering terror of acid
to graze its teeth.

It does not tonight,
and the whole world seems
disappointed at the lack of flair,

the quiet night providing no cradle
for anyone's cheap bravery or full-
throated anarchist dreams.

How hungry we all were and have been
for so long. How hungry we still are.
We regroup and join another crowd

sprawled across another parking lot.
West Florissant sweats, glistens, imagines
we'd all taste better with more salt.

# ON COURTING THE FIRE

The view from below is hazy, footprinted.
Ghost-kin hover just above the gas
as it spreads, thins, fades into the trees.

The air is acidic, many fanged, and unforgiving.
We are gagging, emptying our lungs
of "the humane option," stripping our throats

clean of breath. A police cruiser
is empty and on fire, as are we all,
brandishing our hottest burning things across every street.

Ghost-kin watch us howl, know our mouths
open wide, puffing as we churn our muscles to sprint
up this street and that one.

Each of us a drop
compared to the vastness of legion, of kinfolk,
of ghost-kin with their own jaws cracked wide,

whispering across the tar and grass, the sidewalks
and storefronts, swallowing the feast of a country
having long sowed what can and should come to reaping.

Ghost-kin with scythes, with machetes,
with plows prepared to claw the earth,
having showed us the harvest of generations spilling

out across the land. The view below is hazy,
footprinted but not feared enough. Not feared.
*Not enough*, they say. So we unleash a wall, a fury.

Our kin beckons us, ruffles their skirts,
and shudders their thighs to empty the skyline of smoke.
The ash rises like an offering.

> *Thank you*, they smile,

> *for this*
> *that is so much*
> *less than what is owed us.*

# A LIST OF ITEMS RECOVERED FROM PROTESTERS

*after sam sax*

First, my heart, though covered in dust & peeling
& also the praying palms of someone's mama tucked into a back pocket next to
a sour, sweat-stained kerchief, folded & strained along the diagonal crease
& finally, a rock from the ground of the street that is (still) ours.

First, the praying palms of someone's mama wrapped around a shirt collar
covering a thin gold chain dangling off a bent chest pressed with sweat
& also a rock from the ground of the street that is (still) ours
& finally, a red cap, embroidered with S-T-L in white above the lid.

First, a thin gold chain dangling off a bent chest pressed with sweat;
& also expensive kicks, cheap kicks, knockoffs, flip-flops & boots step-stepping on beat
& also a red cap, embroidered with S-T-L in white above the lid
& finally, a thick grill (the kind that ends up photographed for an edgy gallery, body-less).

First, expensive kicks, cheap kicks, knockoffs, flip-flops & boots step-stepping on beat
to a drum-drum, collecting the bap-baps, the rhythm chants & drumsticks in our fists
& also a thick grill (the kind that ends up photographed for an edgy gallery, body-less)
& finally, the hint of a blunt (a weak strain), dust lingering in the crevice of a pocket.

First, the drum-drum, the bap-baps, the rhythm chants, even without the drumsticks
& also part of a blue-lettered metal tear gas canister, a ghost-home emptied of teeth
& also the hint of a blunt (a weak strain), dust lingering in the crevice of a pocket
& finally, courage, having abandoned metaphor in most cases.

First, part of a blue-lettered metal tear gas cannister
wrapped in a sour, sweat-stained kerchief & folded along the diagonal crease
& also courage, having abandoned metaphor in most cases & becoming
a salve for my heart, though covered in dust & peeling.

# WHAT IS KNOWN AS PARANOIA OR MALADJUSTED SELF-DEFENSE

There is never any warning.
To be honest, I tend to create
the history after the fact,

once the face is shattered,
the bridge full of tumors
and rotting wood. I discover

the long-oozing sore, the burning
path that might suggest
a long-standing infection—

evidence, which here
means: *I am not paranoid;*
*see the line of ash and arson,*

the collapsed metaphors that
might tug the condemnation
free, if only—if only—

but it has always been
this way, without warning.
Suddenly recognizing

no one, and finding
the weapon in all of it.
I am so afraid I am

embarrassed, attacked vividly
somehow by every expression
that creases their lips

to say, I swear, what I know—
*what I know* they must
believe about me, must

see across the glass, the worst
remains—bloodless, heartless,
an old, aging monster

perhaps. I lick my nails
until they glisten, slicing
the light to ribbons, clawing

the faces, the memories,
the open curtains, and
upholstery, shattered glass

between my knuckles. Once
home, I swear, I know
I have defended something—like

myself, perhaps. I coddle
my lonely, rich with isolation,
near gluttonous with it—an excess

of self-absorption probably, but still—
the walls, now six guillotines high,
just as precise and unforgiving,

circle my wet body, supremely naked
and de-skinned, stinging and
joyous, cringing against the cold

air like a newborn or a feral
beast, and suddenly so clean it does not
recognize itself beneath

the moonlight, tiny dots
of blood forming slowly atop
the freshly raw casing,

that skittish layer of under-flesh
that peels its eyes open, stunned
and aware—but calm, finally.

# NAT TURNER COMES TO THE HIGHWAY ACTION

The sun, like a giant heat lamp,
the sky, like a wide blue tarp,
the stretch and stretch
of cars in both directions—
and the people, sitting
anxious before their
steering wheels, vomiting
middle fingers and blaring horns.

I remember the black-gray
pavement like good, good soil
freshly cleared for the planting,
the flickering trail of dancing lights
building in the far-off distance, the line
of us across the highway's waist,
stationed like orange cones except
that when a cone is run over, it does not die.

Nat was there,
imagining the roadway already
planted, pregnant, come to harvest.
He heard a story once
about old, old, old black
magic and a freedom spell.
*Some of the people could fly,* he said,
*And they flew right up out of the fields,*
*up over the gaping white men,*
*black folk pleading with their bones*
*to remember how, all the way*
*back to Africa,* as the story goes.

Nat never saw it, only heard stories,
preferred to privilege his God and deliverance
personally. But here we were, dreaming of sky
and in need of some old, old, old black
magic. He whispered the spell
and some ghosts misted up out of the tar
because, you know, there are bones
everywhere around here—

but for the rest of us, the blue mouth
closed, the people ran, the teeth bit,
and the horror circled, drooled, licked
the air for our fear and surrender.

I remember the chants and all of our proud voices,
the car windows rolled down, and the radio
that tried to swallow us, the uniforms speckling
the freeway's shoulder, the green hillside, the mouth
of badges that began to close around us.

Nat sighed under his breath,
turning his chin up toward the clouds:
*I guess they forgot how.*

He breathed and the roadway breathed
too, promised it would remember us,
said, *the ground holds everything close,*
keeps all the secrets men don't write down.

# WE CALLED IT A "WAR" BECAUSE IT WAS USEFUL, OR ALTERNATE NAMES FOR TEAR GAS

*after Danez Smith*

1. blossoming poison

2. forced abandon (before the handkerchiefs)

3. coward's fire

4. what came without warning, at first

5. the only indictment for miles

6. what came after a warning, eventually

7. America's presumed mercy—which of course dissipates in the wind, which of course,
      is a choking gratitude in the void of massacre, which of course,
      is our most humble foreign policy

8. nightly ghost brand

9. perfume of the streets

10. measured plague & almost certainly someone's evidence of god

11. permissible burning

12. summer baptism at the curb's altar, anointed before heaven
      & hell & everything in between

13. an extended metaphor

14. frontline testimony & bastard badge

15. not water hoses (anymore) at least—which is almost certainly
      a kind of progress,
      no?

# THE STREETLIGHTS CHRISTENED US SAVED (OR AT LEAST SALVAGEABLE)

We start here, at the burnt-orange
streetlight, thrusting the night
into a rust-colored glaze.

All of August is elastic and overstretched,
jumbling the calendar's chronology into a blur.
Last night's string of hours hangs limp,

while tomorrow peels itself across the clock's face.
We start overhead at the burnt-orange
streetlight and wander down to the slow parade

of marchers on the sidewalk, drifting
down West Florissant's length, turning to cross
to the other sidewalk, and drifting back the other way

up the street again. Then another turn
at the far end, the same sidewalk, the same
debris, the same crack a hundred times,

the streetlights' orange hum
battling the shadows' hunger at every turn.
St. Louis's muggy perfume glistens

on our shoulders, in the crook of our arms,
the folded flesh beneath our breasts—a sparse
baptism beneath a handful of electric angels

lighting our small, nightly planet.
Hundreds of bodies churning
the sidewalk's dust to a rhythm,

pulling West Florissant around its own edges.
Here, a whole world in our midst. The gravity
of our heels spins the oceans, presses the tides

forward, shifts entire seasons according to our nightly pace.
A small universe blistering
with smoke and glass,

decade after decade congealing
beneath the streetlights, the burnt-orange
light biting through the night's thick weight,

each fluorescent bulb sharp and persistent
as a single acrylic nail piercing a layer of weave
to disturb the scalp—a pointed green ornament,

generously bedazzled and fighting against the night
for its own color. The burnt-orange light turns the tender
head of flesh into a dome of fading embers

still simmering with color.
The whole street, laced
with a parade of dimly lit orbs

bobbing below the streetlights, circling
relentlessly under threat of arrest, dragging
the street's tiny planet around its axis.

We understood the sunrise
as a distant blessing, the airy blue
morning hue such a strange, thin color

for the streetlights' density
to surrender to. But it is only temporary.
We start here,

at the burnt-orange streetlight, and will end
there, on another night that doesn't yet
know its own name.

# FLATLAND

*for Canfield*

We were obnoxious lovers then.
Loud. Hissing. Fists seeping
through our sun-darkened skin.

A mass of questions marching
across the city, wailing against
the pavement and always returning,

prodigal-like, to the seed of the shattering.
This ravenous freedom: young, brave,
and stubborn. So desperate to see ourselves,

we pressed everything into a mirror,
warped the residential inlet into a shrieking mouth
when the glass broke. We loved you, loved you as we loved

ourselves pressed against phone screens.
Stoop niggas and gold teeth sifted
and strained through protest chants,

a child's bicycle overturned
beneath our urgent, urgent feet.
The bowl of the neighborhood,

a temporary arena, displaced stage
where we bent our shoulders inward, parceled the land
into holy sections. We, audacious and basking in it.

We, drunk on any evidence that someone
like us was alive, still. That the face in the glass
across the bowl of the street had a heartbeat too.

# ON THE CHEMICAL PROPERTIES & USES OF DRIED BLOOD

Months later, West Florissant
is a swollen jaw of chipped teeth.
Its tongue, still stained with
the taste of blood, licks its lips
slowly, reminds itself of
the borders of its own face.

August scratched open
all its throats, stretched the tar
in its skin so tight it pulled
blood out from between
the crevices, from the doorways
of gums & split lips.

Within hours, the whole country's fist
was plunged into its messy gut.
The fingers flexed, began to poke
the warm heat of the pavement.

By November, the fist had retreated & with it, palmfuls of blood:

                       for testing, for study & inspection,
          for research,               for relic,
       for blessing,   for art   &   decoration
              to document,         to share,  to  note
                  its  odd color, to  archive,
                  to display on Instagram, to taste,
             to shine at your friends over coffee,
       to remember, to  remember  &  to  belong.

How useful the bleeding,
how fascinating the shape
a city collapses into after it is drained,
how some bodies are
most recognizable when
there is blood, how some body-cities
are only seen when they are screaming.

In the fist's wake was a hollow,
hand-shaped crevice of scalped air,
so clean that it appeared
at first, as tear gas inverted,
some kind of weird ghost
existing only in the moment
between a freshly launched
canister & its paralyzing bloom.

# FOR THE HOOKED KNIFE

His social media post status said simply:

*Headed into a war zone. Leaving*
*for Ferguson on Saturday.*

The declaration pulled my blood taut
as a flock of crows descended over the city.
The stream of well-wishers
on his Facebook wall twisted my hands

shut, pushed my teeth into a rigid fence.
The righteous shoulders lined up
across my computer screen, whitened and stank,
curdled and soured in their bravado.

Prayers shrieked off-key. The sky began to crack
miles before the horizon, and no angels came.
The people's people became a plague; the street, a buffet;
the sun, a warning; the repetition, a haunting

that still hovers above the sidewalk like low fog.
The breath of a flashback condensed
in the cool evening air, the muscle
memory of chaos floating just below the skin.

The show of it all is both expected
and not. It benefits no one to deny
we saw the mutilation as it happened,
the gnarling of love

into a knot, to pretend the world
we have now is not
the exact promise we built
and coaxed into fruition,

a predictable child we all clamored
to abandon. I marvel now, at this boy
traveling across the country,
searching for a redemptive battleground

that doesn't exist, for a fire he can tell the world
is burning—because he's seen it—and then
go home. Mind the headlines and pack the camera.
Name the mirage after a hero in your own language.

Call St. Louis a firestorm, a wake-up call, proof—
though we just call it home. Mock our pride, the curled *r*
having survived every vowel and sliced its way to the crest
of each brazen word, the hooked knife as defiant

as a flyover city that has shaken its tongue
loose to cackle at the moon every night for months;
the lit face daring us and daring us and daring us
again—


//


In six months, when you recall this, when the carcasses
under your fingernails become an award-winning

something as my city readjusts its jaw,
when you prune your Twitter bio

and are called upon to testify,
do not be surprised when I show up—

shadowed and precise—standing in the corner,
watching you vomit up your own supposed glory—

my fingers relaxed, ten pliable daggers at my side,
my mouth wet and glistening, curled into the hooked knife of a snarl.

# A SERIES OF PROOFS, EXPLAINED

St. Louis, in the wake of carnivores:
    a. is surrounded by so much blood it cannot sleep
    b. is desperate to name each tooth, locate the bite marks
    c. is struggling to recognize the carnage as carnage
    d. is surrounded by so much blood it sleeps to survive

St. Louis, after the taxidermist is done:
    a. is found to be full of broken fingers
    b. is found to be overrun by a species of love previously thought extinct
    c. is found to be most gratifying when splayed and glistening
    d. is found to be quite ugly, but deliciously so

St. Louis, according to simple science:
    a. is a good, clean litmus test
    b. is a palatable case study
    c. is a series of proofs, explained
    d. is a research grant proposal (with new financial backers)

St. Louis, after looking up the definition of *cannibalism*:
    a. shattered every mirror in the city
    b. *removed* every mirror in the city AND
       mailed the entire stack to Congress
    c. shattered every mirror in the city AND
       pulled the shards out of America's back,
       careful to avoid the delicate spine,
       the rope of nerves snaking into its skull
    d. shattered every mirror in the city AND
       upon flipping the whole country over onto its stomach,
       marveled at the limp wrists, the swiveled kneecaps,
       saw that the reflecting glass had severed everything

# SELF-PORTRAIT FRAMED IN LIFE BETWEEN PROTESTS

I know it's Thursday, but the Friday
is tonight & the Monday is tomorrow.
Did you email the meetings? The minutes?
Have you emailed Wednesday is

tomorrow? At 6? PM? At the church with the chairs?
In the basement? After the raid, we moved
the Tuesday to Saturday. Do you know how to get in?
After the raid, we have to be careful. Have you

slept, I mean, charged your phone?
Did you get my email? The email? About
Sunday, the next one. No, it's the next one.
I know it's Wednesday, but the Monday

is tomorrow & we had to push the Thursday
to Friday. The Thursday to Friday. You have
class then? What? What? Oh, I know,
my paper was due last week. It's Thursday,

& we still don't know the agenda. For Saturday,
did you pick up the food? Have you organized?
The? The? Yet? Is it tomorrow yet? Yesterday said
don't forget the emails, the meeting Monday, Sunday &

the paper due at midnight. I sent you a message
on Facebook about coordinating rides, have you? Have
you? Yet? No? Where? It's already Sunday & we need
to know by—

# TERRIBLE AND SO, SO ALIVE

What for the black girls who cut their teeth
      so sharp their gums bleed when they chew?
for the black girls who culled the love out
      cuz it costs too much soft?
for the black girls who drained the damp red blessing
      from their bone marrow to make room for guns?
for the black girls hoping they
      break so they
          can
                stop?
for the black girls who let go of the sun in their lovers'
      cheeks just so they could sleep?
for the black girls who made the nightmare a bed
      so it could rest, too?

What for the black girl who lost her mind on the way
      to getting free and replaced it?
for the black girl who replaced her mind with any
      thing *moving, hungry, breathing,* throat-wet, alive?
for the black girl whose *moving, hungry, breathing*
      keeps her here, but also keeps her every
                          thing for itself?
for the black girl whose throat-wet alive
      eats through the stale death in her fingers,
          (thank you
              —oh, thank you)
          but eats her, too?
for the black girl, headless and alive? Fingerless and alive?
      A whole
          terrible, dripping

   monster, but
          also

   (wow,
        a blessing)


              alive, too?

# HOW THE FIRES GOT MISNAMED

It's a kind of showmanship

to gather the wicks and still be shocked at the blazing mess / offended
the fire dared to become itself / to leap against these tiny man-made items
and eat until ash / How dare it / drink the storefront glass until the parking lots

are a diamond highway / to *crackle, crackle* at the thousands of wide-eyed
creatures, screen-lit and hungry / as they glare through livestream feeds,
unmoving and shocked / watching swarms of heat billow beneath the moonlight,

flex against the night sky like an arrogant, thirsty thing / How dare the
fire want a thing and then eat it whole / How dare it want / while the
thin prayer of a TV camera flickers its own need—a slight twitch

at the corner of its mechanic mouth turns its lips neurotic, wired
by compulsion / and a willingness to gorge itself / It feels
full—of something—when the people watch / even as their teeth

crown around the prayer like a ring of wet fingers / having
dug into the feast of raised hands and burning plastic /
How the nailbeds didn't come back blistered and peeling

and smelling / of tear gas must be a feat of design;
in fact, that's the show / of it all, you know?[1] / How
the sky fell into flame and was turned into a candle

/ for them.

---

[1] What welcome collision—sputtering flames fracturing against the midnight sky / writing the
equation for the bomb / then *oh no, oh god, it worked* / and the decades of ghosts and ash after

# THE ONE WHERE THEY WATCH THE DIRECTOR'S CUT BECAUSE IT HAS AN EDGIER ENDING

What if those who called us thugs and thieves
when they meant monsters and beasts, got to watch each of us
become one? Sharpened teeth filling our mouths—if you can even
call our bulbous, drooling mouths, *mouths*.

Our hard-muscled shoulders twisting into four biceps each,
eight gnarled hand-like things, thirty-five calloused knuckles
like the blunted face of a shot and retired bullet,
having entered and been retrieved bloody
from inside the flesh.

Finally, we are what we are:
seasoned disasters, a crowd of black,
helpless, destructible omens ripping wide gashes
through the civil-minded streets
that keep this country running, burning

the permanence and good faith stored in excess
in case of a too-long winter.
What if those who threatened
to hit protesters with their cars,
to send us (presumably) running

with a stream of bullets actually
broke our flesh open? How absurd
to be disappointed that the wet
leaking from our veins wasn't gasoline
or some corrosive evil eating into the road.

How absurd to stand over us and see
just blood, just warm, dead
human muscle—to kneel down
for a closer look, for each of their ugly,
twitching faces to grin, drooling a little—

so human—with delight.

# SELF-PORTRAIT STANDING IN A FIELD OF TEXT MESSAGES, ALL SENT AND ALL BLOOMING UNANSWERED

The body lingers,
teeters on its heels.
The body is unsure
if its arm is indeed
an arm and not a long

apology. The body kneels
as if in prayer but instead
fingers the dirt, unsettles
a small patch and leaves
the undersoil exposed.

The body mimics the excavation.
The body reaches for the flesh
of its own arm and unscrews
the elbow, twisting the wrinkled
dark brown dome

until it unhinges.
The body lets out a sigh
through the corner opening,
clinches its nails just inside
the sheet of skin to pull

the forearm clean as a skinned lamb.
The body watches the heat
rise from the flesh, red and blurry,
shocking the white bone
cold. The body is pleased

and hungry. The body cleaves
from the elbow again, this time
freeing the bicep, shoulder,
pulling the skin slowly
across the chest—*undt-undt*

goes her heart, suddenly
exposed, the sound
of the body being not
dead zipping out into the world.
The body has a new dilemma:

how to reach the back,
that un-lotioned island
marking her solitude—
which she didn't recognize
until she wasn't alone

and then was again.
The body waits; the body thinks.
The body pulls the face free,
distorting the stretched cheeks
into a swollen, childish pucker

before peeling down
the neck, unsheathing another
shoulder, and then!—with both
top buckles undone, the back flaps
free, steaming vigorously—*undt-undt,*

the body glistens—*undt-undt,*
hisses thickly, the way lungs do,

un-feathered and
wet.

# THE GRILL SHOP AS AN ARMORY

St. Louis is a city
that burned
a night-light into itself.
St. Louis is a mouth
that still has all its teeth
but some of them are
gold, which makes people
not want to hear
it speak or scream
or even laugh.
St. Louis takes
its first deep breath
in months—maybe
years—but they're all so sure
it's just choking,
so sure they freed
its whole big throat—
all them, all of them
from all the way
outside, way out there.
But St. Louis burned
its own night-light
and St. Louis gilded
its own teeth
and St. Louis smiled
without them. It wasn't
choking. It was holding
its breath. It's been blue
with waiting—just held
its breath 'til they all
thought it would die
just to prove
it can survive
anything.

# OH, THE LOVE WE HAD BACK THEN SURVIVED THE SMOKE

When I say
I love you I mean
I got you I mean I don't know
you but do you need a ride? I mean get in
the car for sure I mean hold up you okay? You good?
You need some water you need a charger I mean I got you I mean
wait don't forget to charge your phone don't forget to eat today to get some sleep—

When I say
I love you I mean
watch your back nigga they're coming
up the side street I mean I brought extra Maalox
extra water tilt your head into a stranger's palms I got
you holy baptism in the midst of the fire I mean open your eyes
honey I know it hurts but I got you in the midst of the brimstone too—

When I say
I love you I mean
here are some extra face masks or
you got a scarf or something? Who are you
looking for? Where'd you park can you get to your
car? What's your name I got you I mean I'm scared too I mean
watch your fucking back fam and by fam I mean family or an extended
appendage of this wild beloved thing I mean I recognize you I got you I mean I wrote
the jail support number on my arm for you too—

When I say
I love you I mean
don't throw that and also
fuck it don't say that but also fuck
it I mean we don't say stupid shit like that here nah
no nope homie we don't play that homophobic shit here I love
you and you too I mean I got you and you too I mean I love you too
much to let that slide here—

When I say
I love you I mean
grab him watch him don't let them
pull that shit tonight I mean see those babies
throwing rocks? Watch them I mean help her I got you
get her up I mean make sure she finds somebody she knows
get her some water I mean you can have mine I mean be careful but also fuck it—

When I say
I love you I mean
hold her head hold her head steady
I mean I know honey I know it hurts breathe
steady honey I know breathe I got you you hear me?
I mean open your eyes hon' I know it hurts I mean breathe
honey I mean I got you we got you can you feel my hand under your neck?
Listen to the sound of my voice lean on me and we'll pour it real quick relax I mean
breathe hon' breathe I mean I got you okay how does it feel now? How do you
feel? Can you breathe? Sit up you good? Blink baby blink blink I got you
you good? Can you see? You okay? You? Okay? You? Are you okay?

# HOMEBOUND

When the headlights are still
there twenty minutes later,
my rearview mirror
becomes only this:

two bobbing orbs
wandering lazily around
the slim rectangle of glass
and aluminum anchored
to the roof of my car.

The road lengthens
into a spilled film roll unwinding
in a ribbon across the sky,
ruining its own gift with exposure.

\*

I think of that story from
my childhood about the knife-
wielding killer in the backseat,
the stranger flashing his headlights
to prevent a murder.

\*

There are too many ways home,
so I turn right and choose
another one, turn left and see
the twin beams float around the corner,
slide into the mirrored rectangle again.

\*

The thing about knowing
that you're crazy is that you know.
Instead of your body betraying
you, the illness convinces you to betray
yourself, combing through your biology

for hinges and trapdoors. You mark yourself
unreliable, all paranoia and no grounding,
all rented furniture and no nails in the wall,
no filth in the shape of your body.
It's a thing you live in, but barely.

*

Let's say I don't know other
people who were followed
in those days. Let's say
no one's phones were tapped
and there is no precedent.

*

I remember wanting to call
someone and not knowing who would
believe me. It is the curse of my stupid
body, to believe myself enough to be afraid
but not enough to tell anyone.

*

At some point, people began
measuring political impact
in surveillance. Three
blocked intersections
are worth a single wiretap.

Five weeks of protests equals two.
Three months of direct actions
mean your face thumbtacked
to a corkboard on the wall
of a room you'll never see

the inside of. Any combination
of these may earn an unmarked car.
Hosting protesters from another
city means an undercover
shadow at the next march.

When your phone sputters
in your hands, drops calls,
swallows text messages whole,
you recall the trapdoors, the rented
furniture, the empty walls.

\*

I'm almost home now
and running out
of road, running
out of left turns
and ribbons of faith.

\*

What might be worth a kidnapping?
False imprisonment? It's so stupid
but what might be worth a vanished—?
To disappear someone? My body
is such a stupid body, but

where does my fear go when the ribbon
runs out, when my faith sees
what it sees and still feels ashamed
about the absence? Here, all of
my broken biology again.

\*

Let's say on that night,
it wasn't an officer
flickering around the corner.
Let's say it was
someone else entirely.

\*

When I turn onto the one-way street
below my apartment,
the headlights do not slow
or turn or glare or grimace—

but instead vanish
down the street.

# ALL ASH, AN ANOINTING

When I say that West Florissant is my mind,
I mean, I asked around & everyone thinks it's
broken now & always has been, at least a little.
I mean, I watched the news & every microphone
said, *destroyed*. I mean, I asked the journalists
& the doctors & they both named it *war*.

When I say that West Florissant is a map of my manic episodes,
I mean, remember how the whole street was a giant firework?
How they couldn't look away from the sparks clawing the sky
& laid out blankets to watch? I mean, remember how
stunning the fireball        before it landed? How every riot
is a lightshow        for months        before the ash?

When I say that West Florissant is my bipolar disorder,
I mean that at some point, the arson is both surprise
& expected. I mean that at some point,
everything is ash, isn't & will be again.

When I say that West Florissant is my depression,
I mean that even the ash has a name, has hundreds of them.
I mean that sometimes after a house fire, all you have left
of the carcass is memory, is the knowledge that the residue
of a charred thing still carries a name other than *dust*.
I mean that calling it *all ash* makes lazy work
of what should be called *an anointing*.

# HOW TO MAKE SOUTH GRAND A GHOST TOWN

On this night, the canister
    lands between my feet,
        sprouting a bulbous, billowing white heaven,

empty of harps & mercy,
    void of any god & uninterested
        in finding one.

There is a flash of light,
    a sudden moment when
        the whole world is swallowed

in a bright clap & bang
    & then is remade piece
        by piece in the moonlight.

I'm running & the ground
    appears again, the bits of grass
        sprouting like small, fractured

Edens between the pavement,
    the handful of cars my waist swivels past
        & the night is not over.

The whole world,
    yes, the whole
        world is here.


*//*

The fourth time it happened, I discovered
the body cowers involuntarily, will give up
its senses in exchange for relief
& despite the blinding burn,
will wholly survive.

It is a horribly bearable ruin—
the tinny sour of tear gas,
both handless & choking,
dares your body to escape itself
& empty the skeleton of all its parts

& rid your flesh of mist, this smoke
that brandishes nothing but a stinging
cloud & still lacerates your chest,
spasms your lungs into hard fury
'til the cough & the cough & the cough

& the cough breath the cough & breath
cough cough turns to gag & gag.
Even your kidneys shudder with force.
You think your whole gut has uprooted
& will leave you tonight.

All of this while blinded. All of this
in a noisy darkness that is clamor
& crying & a chorus of throats
all sucking acid until they
find clean air.

You forgot your burning sockets
when your chest ruptured open;
you forgot your chest with all the desperate
gagging; you forgot the gagging while
your eyes drowned themselves

until the acid drowned, too—streamed

down your cheeks
& softened, cooled

your lungs, metronomed
your breathing & released

your eyelids, your fists,
the whole night sky,

so big & finally
visible again.

# AMERICAN FEAR: DIRECTOR'S CUT

One man vomits, his whole body jerking
forward as his last meal surprises
itself out across the pavement, speckling

the toe of his left boot. Another
covers his mouth instinctively,
turns away slightly. Four others

stand up slowly from behind
a police cruiser, forearms buzzing
and weapons alert, their shoulders

rigid with the last four minutes
looping like a circuit wire
through their system.

There is a single siren flickering
around the corner, rushing two
of their own back toward the city.

A woman nudges a fist-sized stone
with her boot, looks blankly
to the line of officers on her left.

One man kneels, lifts the fractured
corner of a brick into his palm,
lets the weight settle into his wrist,

imagines the dent in his helmet,
the bleeding crack above his eye.
He spits. Someone coughs. Another one

reaches into a police cruiser
and unhooks the radio crackling
frantically like a small explosive.

He calls for an ambulance, another one,
*more, help, medical, send them now.*
A woman peels back her helmet

with one hand, revealing a knot
of loose brown curls pinned
to the back of her exposed

head. Someone else coughs,
swallows hard, willing the water
cupped at the edge of his eyelids to stay,

to not sting curved lines
down his cheeks, slivers of [      ]
burning around the border

of his chin before falling
along the heavy lip of his
bulletproof vest.

Farther down the asphalt, people
are sprawled across the
pavement. It's too dark to see

the blood if there's blood.
A few of them shift, whimper.
A man is sobbing so hard

he's choking. One man is kneeling
over someone, shrieking
curses at the flat space of air

in front of him. One woman
doesn't move. The woman
next to her was moving,

but isn't now. Her braids are splayed
across the shimmering asphalt, a half-moon
of knotted rivulets fanning her face.

The moment that lead to this one seems small
now, even smaller still. The men nearest are motionless,
their arms tossed outward or folded

broken beneath them. A Cardinals hat
upturned near a blank skull, having been
emptied and hollowed in the moonlight.

The whole land is a botched experiment, manifest
destiny oozing fresh violences even as it rots.
A country doesn't begin or end on accident.

The strain is a gradual momentum,
but the crack—the snapped neck against the rope
above the crowd—is a sudden and permanent failure,

the cliff's edge our own countrymen kiss
before tumbling over, tugging on their fear like a parachute,
air singing between the loose, loose seams.

Before the massacre, what sharp spasm
of sound?—What bulging pocket
in the shadows?—What cupped

cell phone?—What spiraling debris?—What angel
of rock careening through the sky?—What
monster in the dark?—What imagined threat in my fist?—

What bulbous mass of shrieking chaos?—What bang?—
What pop?—What flash-crack-zing?—What tameless riot
bleeding down the street?—What steady-building

vengeance?—What sleep-deprived bloodthirst?—What well-fed
power trip glaring across the highway?—What string of shouts
spat across the tar?—What feral incivility?—What fear

gave way to this? What fear gave way to this? What fear gave way
to this? What fear gave way to this? What fear gave
way to this? Which way to this? Which fear gave

way to this? What fear gave way to this? What
fear gave way to this? What fear? What fear gave way
to this? Which way to this? Which way? What fear gave

way to this? What fear gave way to this? Fear gave way to this.
But which one? Which fear? Which? What fear gave
way? What? What fear? What fear gave to this? What

fear gave way to this? What fear gave? What fear
gave? What fear gave? What gave us this? What fear? Which
one? Which one? Which fear? What fear gave way? To this?

Which way to this? Which way to this? The fear that gave?
This? Which fear gave this? Which?
What fear? Gave? To this? All of this?

# OBSCENITIES, BUT AS A PRAYER

Opposite the police station,
a ravenous crowd seethes,
human-like, beast-like, full
of blood, of blood, of blood—alive
and daring anyone to doubt
otherwise.

# DRIPPING VILLANELLE FOR THE BURNED WALGREENS, QUIKTRIP, PRIME BEAUTY, ET AL.

When the fire blazes, it blazes with might!
*Oh no*, they say, *the bricks & things!*
as the storefronts—the storefronts!—crumble in light.

The plastic signs wilt & curl in the night,
while for hours in St. Louis, the sirens still ring,
as the fire blazes & blazes with might.

How foolish to tempt & yet be shocked at the sight,
as we prove what anger (& love) again brings,
as the storefronts—the storefronts!—crumble in light.

News headlines mourn the losses of the fight
(aisles of burned chips, gum & packaged eyelash wings)
as the fire blazes & blazes with might.

The cameras capture the chaos & fists wrung tight.
*So reckless, the wild rioters!* the suit-and-ties sing,
as the storefronts—the storefronts!—crumble in light.

Yet how subdued the blaze when considered it's quite
a muted response to the life-stealing & stealing & stealing & stealing & stealing & stealing
When the fire blazes & blazes with might,
as the storefronts—the storefronts!—crumble in light.

& stealing
& stealing
& stealing
& stealing

—& stealing that stings

# ULCER (WITH FOOTNOTES)

*In response to a 2015 performance poem repurposing Michael Brown's autopsy*

In this one, he writes the same poem[1]
about Michael Brown's autopsy,
pulling the bones up out of the bleach
and splaying the wet bounty across a thick
metal table, a string of footnotes
lolling off the page's bottom lip
like a row of confetti-ed news stories
brightening under a harsh and hungry light.

In this one, he writes the same
poem[2] and instead of the QuikTrip,
someone douses a stack of canonized texts
in flame, the pages roaring in protest
against their charred and curled edges—
maybe that or some other nightmarish
destruction that poets grieve in theory.

In this one, he writes the
same poem[3] and the lining
of my stomach begins to curdle.
The theory is the world is burning
and so might the books; the theory is
to save the books, we burn something
else; the theory is anything
can be fodder for almost anything.

In this one, he writes
the same poem[4], and my body retches
across the stage, covers the microphone
in the blood-wet applause of last night's dinner,
reverse burial, the machine's gears
click-clicking the casket back up
into the hungry, hungry world again.

---

[1] How small and wanting to experiment
    into the void of another life;
[2] how gratuitous the gaping mouth,
    the loud, gnawing hunger-wonder in the direction
[3] of someone else's grief because art.
[4] Because.

# I BEND AND THE TENDER JOINT BUCKLES

In the softest part of my body,
just below the dipped angle
of my pelvis, in the warm crease
before the bubble of my thigh,

the layers of violence pickle
and soften my wrinkled flesh.
The scattered tilework of recollection
brings Ferguson back into focus,

the thin sheath of distanced metaphor
thrusts my raw nerves back toward
memory's softened front gate.
This, such an intimate survival,

a particular sprawling of grief
the whole world remembers watching
from a distance, the violence dimpling
into soft rivulets of haunted air.

Years later, my softest flesh murmurs
against the news current, hiccups
impolitely at the dissonance
fracturing across the headlines.

For every burning trashcan
and flipped car after a football game,

                              the soft place.


For every international upheaval coaxing
the milky lull of liberal applause,

                              the soft place.


For every headline that flickers with metaphor
and memory piercing my lungs,

                              the soft place.

For every flashback that balks halfway
up my throat and nests there in the darkness,

                                   the soft place.

For every comparison that draws its outline,
shrieking at its own silhouette in the mirror,

                                   the soft place.

I bend and the tender joint buckles softly,
humming against itself, humming everything I did
not say, did not pierce and spill, did not break;
everything I could've violently taken,

scraped roughly across the horizon
and thrown against the soft, starved Earth;
all the fear, all that time; the curses
I swallowed, the stinging sour that burns

still; every time I did not when I should've,
every violent shattering I kept palmed in my fist.
It's a soft and selfish thing, flailing and dark
and dense with life. You're welcome.

For keeping it
here, creviced,

instead of.

# KINDLING

There is a black man I know
who wants me fractured
and feast-able for the flame.

I know because he told me so.
Pressing the sun into my teeth, he tells me
I am lucky for the warmth, that I carry the soot

so lightly on my lips and eyelashes,
so graceful I am with the scalded skin
webbing across my back.

Today, I am broken,
collapsed and balancing only
on the thin anchor of my heels.

Having spent years making a crown
of my own forgiveness, he tells me
to cover myself in ash for him—

all the while, my bones are flecking away
in the heat, shimmering into orange sparks
that refuse the body if they cannot be whole.

But he still asks me for this—me, now body-less,
hot, and swirling. Despite both our houses
turned to kindling, despite the cloud smoke,

the clogged lungs dusted with the charred remnants
of a whole thing, he still says *burn for me* like a lost boy
searching for the sunrise by burning down the sky.

//

There is a black man I know
who is jealous of the way
I can be consumed. He tells me,

*The way white men hunger*
*after the dream of your body*
*breaking between their palms*

*means you will always exist—even if*
*only between someone else's teeth.*
My jaw slips askew, loosens

into a monstrous, gaping wound
that will flood itself to fill every void.
Can I not be more than carcass?

If I am to be edible, let me fill
the gut with rage and rot. Watch me
bring ruin with my limbs attached.

I will loose all the injury
and it will coat the whole world
and I will become a spigot

for all my most careful survivals.
I will loose my tongue and instead
I will eat and eat and eat and enjoy it.

I am learning the forsaken also forsake others
and before I weep for him, I will show him
what I have learned to become
        when men try to swallow me whole.

//

Hallelujah for our matching, combustible
throats. Hallelujah for the wild exhaustion
that has left us desperate for fire. Hallelujah
for the fire, I love you. Hallelujah for my
arms, I love you, the kindling. For the
kindling's ability to feed everything.
For everything to be able to eat me,
I love you. Hallelujah, that you expect
me boundless, ever a thing you are
most grateful for after I am ash.
Here, the sun in my teeth because
unity, because you think, hallelujah, *black
women were made to bleed in exchange
for this.* My sternum cracked in the heat
for this, I love you. Hallelujah, I'm so tired,
beloved, I do not owe you a martyr.
My flesh is a not a hearth for your teeth.
Hallelujah, you will not make a home
of me. To demand myself body
rather than metaphor is not selfish.
Hallelujah, your violence is not
an heirloom. It is the thing—after
the whole house is gone, after
the clouds have gorged themselves
on smoke and soot—that the fireman
will lean over, pointing: there,
there is where it began.

# IT DIDN'T RAIN MUCH THAT AUGUST, BUT AFTER

St. Louis is a pretty city, pretty like the sudden crack-yelp of thunder
across the daylit May sky, shimmying out a sweeping gray sheet of shattered

cloud like a frantic slap of ocean wave ran through a city-sized sifter,
lapping wildly at the broken sidewalk, tossing the twisting storm sideways

through the muggy landscape before sputtering to its knees like a stumbled
stampede, coughing out the sun's shoulders, collarbone, neck—

> sweetly, the damp eyelids
> of the trees moan and blink, gazing
> at the oversaturated world around it,
> having soaked up itself and feasted
> freely on the water and its own density,
> its own skin and hair—St. Louis flesh
> and bone, wet and milky with its
> own green and gray softness, thickly colored,
> decaying brick and French-inspired,
> cement-lipped archways and stoops
> lining the state streets like a lattice
> of zippers opening and closing on the city's
> Southside—

then the chin, bubble of lips, two cheekbones, and the whole burning,
distant thing, alive and scorching, stealing the wetness

from the puddle-rich sidewalk, air-drying the fertile forest of low-rise city
bracing against the rising humidity come late St. Louis summer:

*so hot I can't believe we;*
*remember the bottled water by the;*
*booooyyyy that sticky ass;*
*marching in a loop-de-loop like a;*
*muhfuckas wouldn't even let us stop to—*

> There was a before, I swear; there was
> a during, I swear; there is an—

# PICK ONE, IT SAYS

1. After a nightmare:

On a cool night empty of moon, my mind reshuffles its terror
into a fresh swatch of colors fanned across my eyelids.

*Pick one,* it says, as I fall asleep, my skin, a kaleidoscope
of leaking holes. I think, *Yes, this makes sense.*

*Some days there is a whole ankle lodged in my throat,*
*toenails digging into my kidneys, dragging my torso across the city.*

*Some days my body reshuffles itself to get a better view,*
*streamlines the blood flow with a new current.*

*Don't worry—in this version you survive but without your collarbone—in this version*
*you do survive but hairless, skinless, breathless—in this version you still survive but*

*dismembered, your legs there and there, your elbows there and there, an eye socket*
*rolled here, your pelvis shattered there—in this version you survive and swallow*

*the meetings the hours the marches exhausted the tears the gas the laughter*
*the dead phones and lost friends behind the trees but the police line*

*looked like it was moving toward the mouth of the parking lot and there's a fence*
*back here y'all there's a fence back here we can't get out this way they'll kill*

*us they'll kill us run not that way run come here they're gonna go behind*
*that building and block the alley off they're blocking the alley go go did you see*

*where he went I can't find can't find him can't find him go go go come here call me*
*when you get call me when call me when you*
> *—get to the car*
> > *—can charge your phone*
> > > *—get back home      safe.*

2. After a nightmare, the body responds:

Don't be mad

at me for this.

It is a gift,

to watch the terror

congeal in your sleep

and see you

survive it

again.

Look at you,

shocked upright

in your bed

by your own

screams.

Look at you,

sobbing the abyss

off your skin.

Look at you,

all terrified

and still here.

# BRICK-MADE AND STEADY

St. Louis. St. Louis. St. Lou-Lou-Lou. St. Louiiis-iiiiiis.
Saint! Saint! Saint Lou! She's a saint, ain't—

ain't she? Saint of trees and rolling, wide green.
Saint of the lost-lost and goings. Shepherd of the Miss-Mississip-

Mississippi River's exit and the Missouri River's southern soup,
dark and thick as love's messy wander, broad and swirling as a feast

flooding the void of an empty belly, blue-gray with migration
and so many feet and family grinding up the river toward something—

Saint Loouuuu! North-south Saint Louis, blue-green St. Lou.
St. Lou-St. Lou-St. Lou. A ho-hum hungry, beloved.

Beloved, beloved Midwest, wide and sprawling, grin-wide country,
pig-feet country, can't pronounce the French street names country,

upper chin of the south, land of the loose-lipped *r* clutching its vowels close,
wild west and still middle best Saint Lou. My saint of loss and desire,

of growing and long-suffering beauty in her bricks,
in her humidity-soaked skin, brown and burned in the middle,

in the middle—my Saint, crowning above the country's heart,
a birth sweet and bloodied. Pinched city at the state line

and fanning west with flight and flutter, brick-made
and steady as the seasons, which maybe isn't saying much

nowadays, but St. Lou-St. Lou—my beloved—my bastard and my treasure.
St. Lou-Lou-Lou, my heart-sick, heart-hungry beacon

salivating at the moon's dogged persistence, ready always
to bare its teeth at the sky's heedless blue

and gather our dark brown lips, ready to spit and dance,
ready to flicker over language like a country spell

and deliver anyone's sins back to them on beat, to a rhythm,
with a choir of shimmying jaws laughing at each note.

Louis moans and croons like only Louis knows how,
a saint with blue notes in its skin, tinted like an evening hue,

having flooded the evening with a nighttime of knuckles
braced against the horizon's mouth for months and months

and months and yet still honeyed, still sweetened
with local flavor, spiced generously with home.

## STILL UNBUTTONED & UNBOTHERED: ON IMAGINING THAT FREEDOM PROBABLY FEELS LIKE GETTING *THE ITIS*

The table settles. Before you
is a series of well-seasoned scraps
framed in silverware and open
palms. The entire kitchen
exhales and every torso
leans back in unison, a table
blossoming bodies in satisfaction.
Someone pops open a button,
and then another. Several burps
that interrupt, scoff at the hand
cupped around the mouth,
bellow with pleasure
as they fling out of the body
in triumph. Every bra is undone
unceremoniously, straps wilting
out of shirt sleeves or across furniture.
The land of satiation. The land of, *if it itches,*
*scratch it.* Land of pleasure. Everything
sagging with joy. Someone passes gas
loudly. It is full and foul, but no one
is embarrassed by the scent
of a body that has gotten exactly
what it needed.

        The stench of enough.

My god, to be so satisfied you reek of it.

Smell badly of, *I do not want more,*
*I have had my fill.* To stink of gratitude,
to be immobilized by its weight. The eyelids
flutter, nearly drunk with it. Here, the body
so saturated and somehow fears
nothing. What a condition
for the body, so unlike
the state I am in. So enough
that all it must do
is sleep.

# ACKNOWLEDGMENTS

Gratitude to the editors and poetry readers of the following journals and platforms in which versions of these poems first appeared, sometimes under different titles:

*Anomaly*: "Flatland," "We Called It A 'War' Because It Was Useful, or Alternate Names for Tear Gas," and "What Is Known as Paranoia or Maladjusted Self-Defense"

*Blueshift Journal*: "A Series of Proofs, Explained"

*Drunk in a Midnight Choir*: "On the Chemical Properties & Uses of Dried Blood"

*Green Mountains Review*: "Dripping Villanelle for the Burned Walgreens, Quik-Trip, Prime Beauty, et al."

*Grub Street*: "Self-Portrait Framed in Life between Protests" and "Self-Portrait Standing in a Field of Text Messages, All Sent and All Blooming Unanswered"

*The Minnesota Review*: "A List of Items Recovered from Protesters" and "For the Street That Held Us"

*River Styx*: "By the Grace of the Gaze"

*The Rumpus*: "How the Fires Got Misnamed," "Terrible and So, So Alive," and "Ulcer (with Footnotes)"

*Tinderbox Poetry*: "How to Make South Grand a Ghost Town"

*Underblong*: "All Ash, An Anointing"

"Pick One, It Says" was selected by Ilya Kaminsky for the 2020 James H. Nash Poetry Prize

"STILL UNBUTTONED & UNBOTHERED: On Imagining That Freedom Probably Feels Like Getting *the Itis*" was selected by Fatimah Asghar to be featured in the Academy of American Poet's Poem-A-Day series

Thank you to St. Louis for keeping me rooted all these years, for holding me while I grew into myself, and for all the ways you've let me make a home here.

Thank you to Ariana Brown and Sasha Banks for your sisterhood, for the day we sat on a hotel room bed in Illinois and laughed and dreamed, for loving me deliberately, and for helping me recognize myself again. To Angela Goodiel and Elizabeth Jordan for staying all this time and for being by my side when I needed you. To Jonathan Fenderson for your guidance and for walking me toward the histories and principles that still ground my politics today.

Thank you to Fred Reeder for believing in my poems, for teaching me to love language and to learn the rules so that I could break them. To Justin Phillip Reed and DeShara Suggs-Joe for reading the draft version of this with care. To Sam Gaitsch, Dalychia Saah, Leslie Salisbury, and Camille Wright for being so generous with your time and your patience, so steady with your love and your friendship.

Thank you to WU-SLam and squids (forever). To Mimi Borders, Kate Hao, Kristen Sze-Tu, and Kris Tavassoli, for the poems you were brave enough to write and let me edit with you. To BEOTIS, for the flowers, always.

To Pacia Anderson, Shine Goodie, Cheeraz Gorman, and Treasure Shields-Redmond, thank you for opening your arms so wide to me and my poetry and telling me I belonged here more than a decade ago. To all of the people who have been so generous with their hugs the few (and still fewer) times I've left my house in recent years, I cannot thank you enough. To all the people who have extended me an abundance of grace and kindness, especially these last few years; I cannot thank you enough either. To anyone who has told me they loved me and meant it and has not waivered since, thank you immensely for that gift.

To my protest family; to the friends and strangers who ran Action Council meetings, led medic trainings, sent emails, organized supplies, and staffed jail support; to St. Marks, the World Community Center, KB Frazier's drums, and "the Assata chant"; to MJ Johnson, Jonathan Karp, Hezekiah McCaskill, Clark Randall, LaKeyra Stephens, Maya Walton, Jarris "J.J." Williams, and the St. Louis Students in Solidarity; to everyone who made up the uprising, to all of us—what is there even to say? The world would not be what the world is today without all of us. We broke and we bent and we built. We stayed and we fought. Can you believe the audacity, to be brave and imperfect, to fill the streets and refuse to move? How does one honor that kind of steady, traumatic, righteous defiance? How does one heal from it? Who loves our city bigger than us? No one.

# ABOUT CAAPP

The mission of the Center for African American Poetry and Poetics (CAAPP) is to highlight, promote, and share the work of African American and African diasporic poets and to pollinate cross-disciplinary conversation and collaboration. Housed at the University of Pittsburgh, CAAPP's programming aims to present live poetry and conversation, contextualize the meaning of that work, and archive it for future generations.

The Center emerged in a 2015 brainstorming session between poets Dawn Lundy Martin, Terrance Hayes, and Yona Harvey, and was officially founded in 2016. Today, the Center is a space for innovative collaboration between writers and other artists, scholars, and social justice activists thinking through poetics as a unique and contemporary movement. In its effort to highlight, promote, archive, research, and generally advance the practices and epistemologies of African American and African diasporic poetry and poetics, CAAPP supports individual writers, artists, scholars, and others nationally and at a range of career stages and academic ranks. The Center also prioritizes providing opportunities for poets and artists outside of academia, in the Pittsburgh community and beyond.

# ABOUT THE CAAPP BOOK PRIZE

Started in 2020, the CAAPP Book Prize is a publishing partnership between CAAPP and Autumn House Press with the goal of publishing and promoting a writer of African descent. The prize is awarded annually to a first or second book by a writer of African descent and is open to the full range of writers embodying African and African diasporic experiences. The book can be of any genre that is, or intersects with, poetry, including poetry, hybrid work, speculative prose, and/or translation.

# NEW AND FORTHCOMING

*Seed Celestial* by Sara R. Burnett
Winner of the 2021 Autumn House Poetry Prize, selected by Eileen Myles

*Bittering the Wound* by Jacqui Germain
Winner of the 2021 CAAPP Book Prize, selected by Douglas Kearney

*The Running Body* by Emily Pifer
Winner of the 2021 Autumn House Nonfiction Prize, selected by Steve Almond

*Entry Level* by Wendy Wimmer
Winner of the 2021 Autumn House Fiction Prize, selected by Deesha Philyaw

*The Scorpion's Question Mark* by J. D. Debris
Winner of the 2022 Donald Justice Poetry Prize, selected by Cornelius Eady

*Given* by Liza Katz Duncan
Winner of the 2022 Rising Writer Prize in Poetry, selected by Donika Kelly

*Ishmael Mask* by Charles Kell

*Origami Dogs: Stories* by Noley Reid